MW01100839

DEC   2012

Canada's Political Parties

THE
LIBERAL
PARTY

Douglas and Patricia Baldwin

Weigl

Published by Weigl Educational Publishers Limited
6325 10th Street SE
Calgary, Alberta
T2H 2Z9

Website: www.weigl.ca

Library and Archives Canada Cataloguing in Publication

Baldwin, Douglas, 1944-
          Liberal Party / Douglas and Patricia Baldwin.

(Canada's political parties)
Includes index.
ISBN 978-1-77071-697-1 (bound).--ISBN 978-1-77071-702-2 (pbk)

          1. Liberal Party of Canada. I. Baldwin, Patricia, 1946-
II. Title. III. Series: Canada's political parties (Calgary, Alta.)

JL197.L5B35 2011   j324.27106   C2011-900817-3

Printed in the United States of America in North Mankato, Minnesota
1 2 3 4 5 6 7 8 9 0 15 14 13 12 11

072011
WEP040711

Project Coordinator: Heather Kissock
Design: Terry Paulhus

Photograph Credits
CP Images: pages 17TL, 17TR, 18, 20, 21BR, 25BL; Dreamstime: page 4; Getty Images: pages 7, 9BL, 9BR, 10, 11TR, 11BL, 13BL, 13BR, 14, 15TL, 15BL, 15BR, 16, 17BL, 19, 21TL, 21TR, 21BL, 22M, 22B, 23T, 24TL, 24TM, 24M, 24B, 25TR, 25M, 26, 27; iStockphoto: page 15TR; Library and Archives Canada: pages 6, 8, 9TL, 9TR, 11TL, 11BR, 12, 13TL, 13TR, 17BR, 22T, 23B, 24TR, 25TL.

Every reasonable effort has been made to trace ownership and to obtain permission to reprint copyright material. The publishers would be pleased to have any errors or omissions brought to their attention so that they may be corrected in subsequent printings.

We acknowledge the financial support of the Government of Canada through the Canada Book Fund for our publishing activities.

CONTENTS

Overview of Canada's Political Parties 4

The Liberal Party—Its Beliefs and Philosophy 5

Liberal Party Leaders 6

The Early Years, 1867–1896 8

Years of Success, 1896–1911 10

Reshaping Canada, 1921–1948 12

Post-War Politics, 1948–1967 14

The Exciting Years, 1968–1984 16

The Chrétien Years, 1990–2003 18

The Years in Exile, 2003–2011 20

Timeline 22

10 Fast Facts About the Liberal Party 24

Activity 26

Quiz 28

Further Research 30

Glossary 31

Index 32

Overview of Canada's Political Parties

Political parties in Canada are made up of people with similar beliefs who have joined together to accomplish specific goals. To achieve these goals, the party attempts to elect enough members to gain control of the government.

Political parties are central to our political system. In their attempts to win elections, parties propose a series of social, economic, and political policies called the party platform. The election campaign then attempts to convince the people to vote for candidates who support these beliefs. This process provides the people with a way of expressing their opinions and of holding the winning party accountable for its actions.

Beginnings

The first Canadian political parties started in central Canada in the late 1700s. They were created to ensure that the people's wishes were presented to the British governor who ruled the **colonies**. The achievement of **responsible government** in the late 1840s paved the way for the emergence of party politics as we know it today. When Canada became a nation in 1867, there was only the Liberal Party and the Conservative Party. These two parties dominated politics until the 1920s. The rise of the Progressive Party in the 1920s, and the emergence of the Co-operative Commonwealth Federation and the Social Credit parties in the 1930s gave voters more choices through which to express their concerns. However, these "third" parties never seriously challenged the power of the two major parties.

This situation changed, however, in the 1980s. The Reform Party began in 1987 as an alternative to the Progressive Conservative Party. In 2000, it transformed into the Canadian Alliance, which then merged with the Progressive Conservative Party in 2003 to form the Conservative Party. Today, the Conservative Party, Liberal Party, New Democratic Party (NDP), Green Party, and Bloc Québécois compete to dominate Canadian politics.

In Canada, federal, provincial, and municipal governments discuss and make decisions about many activities that affect the daily lives of citizens.

🍁 The Parliament Buildings in Ottawa have been the centre of Canadian politics since 1867.

The Liberal Party—
Its Beliefs and Philosophy

The Liberal Party has gone through several major philosophical phases. Traditionally, the party has supported individual liberty, **representative government**, and limited restrictions on the economy. Edward Blake and Wilfrid Laurier, for example, pushed for free trade with the United States. Beginning with William Lyon Mackenzie King, the party passed social welfare legislation for the less fortunate. Later leaders, including Lester Pearson and Pierre Trudeau, pushed for justice for all peoples, a regulated economy, and **diplomacy** in foreign affairs.

Specific policies change from year to year and are a critical part of all parties. Each party allows its members to assist in policymaking. This usually occurs at national party conventions, where members can introduce, debate, and vote on policies.

The Liberal Constitution

A party's constitution is a formal document that outlines its basic beliefs and principles. Following is part of the preamble to the Liberal constitution.

"The Liberal Party of Canada is dedicated to the principles that have historically sustained the Party: individual freedom, responsibility and human dignity in the framework of a just society, and political freedom in the framework of meaningful participation by all persons. The Liberal Party is bound by the constitution of Canada and to the pursuit of equality of opportunity for all persons, to the enhancement of our unique and diverse cultural community, to the recognition that English and French are the official languages of Canada, and to the preservation of the Canadian identity in a global society."

Registering a Political Party

1. Political parties do not have to be registered with the government. However, registered parties can provide tax receipts for donations, thus saving the donors money. An official party can place its name beneath its candidates' names on the ballot.

2. To be registered, a party must:
- Have statements from at least 250 individuals who are qualified to vote (i.e. 18 years old and a Canadian citizen) indicating that they are party members
- Endorse at least one candidate in a general election or a by-election
- Have at least three officers, in addition to the party leader, who live in Canada and are eligible to vote
- Have an auditor
- Submit a copy of the party's resolution appointing its leader
- Have an agent who is qualified to sign contracts
- Submit a letter stating that the party will support one or more of its members as candidates for election

3. The party's name, abbreviation, or logo must not resemble those of any other party and must not include the word "independent." Once the Chief Electoral Officer has verified the party's application (confirming that 250 electors are members of the party and that the party has met all the other requirements), and is satisfied that the party's name and logo will not be confused with those of another registered or eligible party, he or she will inform the party leader that the party is eligible for registration.

Source: Elections Canada

Liberal Party Leaders

The Liberal Party has been a dominant political party in Canada since before Confederation. Through the course of its history, the party has won many federal elections, and, as a result, several of its leaders have assumed the position of prime minister.

Liberal Party Leaders	
NAME	TERM
George Brown	1861-72
Alexander Mackenzie	1873-80
Edward Blake	1880-87
Wilfrid Laurier	1887-1919
Daniel D. McKenzie	1919
William Lyon Mackenzie King	1919-48
Louis St. Laurent	1948-58
Lester B. Pearson	1958-68
Pierre Trudeau	1968-84
John Turner	1984-90
Herb Gray	1990
Jean Chrétien	1990-2003
Paul Martin	2003-06
Bill Graham	2006
Stéphane Dion	2006-08
Michael Ignatieff	2008-2011
Bob Rae	2011-

FIRST PARTY LEADER
GEORGE BROWN (1818-1880)

George Brown was the owner of the *Toronto Globe*, and a prominent Toronto businessman. He was first elected to the legislature in 1851 and, in 1857, took on the job of reorganizing the Clear Grit, or Liberal, Party. Brown was a supporter of representation by population and one of the Fathers of **Confederation**.

George Brown died tragically after he was shot by an employee he had fired.

FIRST LIBERAL PRIME MINISTER
ALEXANDER MACKENZIE 1822-1892

When Mackenzie's father died in Scotland in 1835, Alexander quit school and took a job as a stonemason to support his family. Seven years later, he came to Canada. In 1861, he was elected to the government and slowly rose in the party ranks. As prime minister, Mackenzie oversaw the completion of the Parliament Buildings in Ottawa. Mackenzie remained a Member of Parliament until his death in 1892.

Alexander Mackenzie was offered a knighthood three times. He refused each one, citing his working class roots.

SEVENTH PRIME MINISTER
WILFRID LAURIER 1841-1919

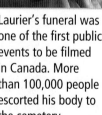

Laurier was born in St. Lin, Quebec. When he was 11 years old, his father sent him to school in the neighbouring town of New Glasgow to learn English. At school, Laurier became fascinated with politics and the law. He became a lawyer in Montreal and, in 1874, was elected to the House of Commons. Laurier's elegant speeches and pleasant personality won people over. As a result, he won the elections of 1896, 1900, 1904, and 1908. The issue of **conscription** in World War I divided Canadians and turned many English friends against him. In the 1917 election, the Liberal Party was massacred. Two years later, Laurier died of a stroke.

Laurier's funeral was one of the first public events to be filmed in Canada. More than 100,000 people escorted his body to the cemetery.

FOURTEENTH PRIME MINISTER
LESTER BOWLES PEARSON
1897-1972

Lester B. Pearson was known as both an academic and an athlete. After receiving his Master of Arts in history at Oxford University, he joined the history department at the University of Toronto in 1923. He went to work for the federal government when the Department of External Affairs hired him in 1928. In 1948, Pearson entered the House of Commons. In 1956, a military conflict erupted for control of the Middle East's Suez Canal. Pearson's idea of an international peacekeeping force led by Canadian troops captured the day. For this, he was awarded the Nobel Peace Prize in 1957. He was elected Canada's prime minister six years later. Lester Boyles Pearson died of cancer in 1972.

Pearson's nickname was Mike. He was given this name by his wartime flight instructor, who felt that Lester was an unsuitable name for a soldier.

FIFTEENTH PRIME MINISTER
PIERRE ELLIOTT TRUDEAU
1919-2000

Pierre Elliott Trudeau was born in Montreal. He earned his law degree at the Université de Montréal and later studied at Harvard and in Europe. Pearson appointed Trudeau minister of justice in 1967. He became prime minister in 1968, holding the position for most of the next 16 years. In his last years, Trudeau suffered from Parkinson's disease and prostate cancer. He died in 2000.

Trudeau was known being debonair and flamboyant. He drove a Mercedes-Benz sports car, wore capes and big hats, and often had a red rose in his lapel.

TWENTIETH PRIME MINISTER
JEAN CHRÉTIEN
1934-

Jean Chrétien was born in Quebec, to working-class parents. As a boy, he attended political rallies with his father. By the time he was 15, he was campaigning for Liberal candidates. Chrétien was elected to the House of Commons in 1963. He became leader of the Liberal Party in 1990. Three years later, he became prime minister, a post he held until his retirement in 2003.

Chrétien often referred to himself as "the little guy from Shawinigan" to note his small-town roots.

🍁 The newly formed Liberal Party combined English and French Canadian reformers in one political unit.

The Early Years, 1867–1896

It was not until 1861 that the Liberal Party was officially established in central Canada.

The origins of the Liberal Party trace back to the reformers of the 1820s and 1830s. These people fought for greater **democracy** in the colonies and opposed the concept of a ruling class. They believed that responsible government was the only way to give all Canadians the same rights.

The reformers were able to form a government in the mid 1800s, and achieved responsible government during their time in office. However, in the years that followed, the political landscape began to change, and the reform movement dissipated.

The Liberal Party was not officially established until 1861. When the party's first leader, George Brown, failed to win his seat in the first Canadian election in 1867, Alexander Mackenzie became Liberal leader.

From Confederation until 1896, except for one brief period, the Conservative Party dominated the House of Commons. Thanks to the **Pacific Scandal**, the Liberals under Alexander Mackenzie formed the first Liberal government in 1873.

Unfortunately for Mackenzie, Canada was in the midst of an **economic depression**, which the voters blamed on the government. The Liberals lost the 1878 election to John A. Macdonald. Mackenzie remained party leader until Edward Blake replaced him in 1880. Blake, a Toronto lawyer and ex-premier of Ontario, led the party until Wilfrid Laurier assumed control in 1887.

A RAILWAY TO THE WEST

During his term in office, Prime Minister John A. Macdonald was committed to building a railway that would unite the country from east to west. In fact, it was the promise of the railway that convinced British Columbia to join Confederation. When Alexander Mackenzie became prime minister, the government's priorities shifted, with Mackenzie questioning the necessity of the railway.

YES TO CONSTRUCTION

Macdonald and his supporters agreed that building a transcontinental railway would encourage settlement in the West and unify the country. This was especially important as the United States had just bought Alaska from Russia and was expressing interest in Canada's western lands. Settlement would ensure the land remained Canadian.

NO TO CONSTRUCTION

Mackenzie thought that building a transcontinental railway to British Columbia was too expensive an undertaking. There were very few people living in British Columbia at the time and very few people travelled from Ontario to the Pacific Ocean, so there was no rush to link the West to the East.

THE RESULT

The dispute over the railway's construction became so heated that British Columbia threatened to leave Canada. The governor general had to intervene in order to settle the dispute and continue the plans for the railway. Despite Mackenzie's objections, during his tenure as prime minister, 4,000 kilometres of railway tracks were laid. The construction of the Canadian Pacific Railway was completed in 1885.

Liberal Legacy

The Liberal Party achieved much during its four years in office.

1. It established the Supreme Court.
2. The Liberal Party replaced open voting with the secret ballot.
3. It established *Hansard*, the written record of the House of Commons debates.
4. The Liberal Party founded the Royal Military College.
5. It established the post office to deliver mail door-to-door in the major cities.

The Royal Military College was founded in Kingston, Ontario, in 1874. It admitted its first cadets two years later.

Canada's Supreme Court is the country's highest court. Legal cases that could not be settled in provincial or territorial courts are decided here.

Years of Success, 1896–1911

Wilfrid Laurier was a surprise choice as leader in 1887. Many in the party considered him too frail and easygoing to be an effective leader. Nine years later, Laurier became the first French-Canadian prime minister of Canada and successfully led the party to victories in 1900, 1904, and 1908.

Laurier fought to keep French and English-Canadian disagreements from splitting the nation apart. He was especially tested, however, when Great Britain asked Canada to contribute money to its navy. Laurier knew that if he provided the money, as English Canadians wanted, he would offend French Canadians, who were against any involvement in European conflicts.

Laurier compromised. He proposed to create a Canadian navy that could be loaned to Great Britain if needed. In a fierce debate in the House of Commons, French Canadians accused Laurier of giving in to the British. Laurier's hold on the people of Quebec began to slip.

The next year, Laurier promised a **reciprocity** agreement with the American government. To his surprise, reciprocity was not popular with many Canadians. Manufacturers feared that American products would be cheaper and thus undersell them. The Conservative Party accused Laurier of giving away Canada's economic and political independence. The twin issues of reciprocity and Canada's navy brought Laurier's downfall. In 1911, Robert Borden became prime minister.

> **Laurier fought to keep French and English-Canadian disagreements from splitting the nation apart.**

🍁 The British government wanted Canada to help fund the construction of several dreadnoughts. These were the "super battleships" of the time.

CREATING A CANADIAN NAVY

By 1909, Great Britain feared that the growing strength of Germany's navy was a threat to its trade and military security. Britain asked Canada to help it keep pace with Germany by contributing money to construct dreadnoughts. Faced with a difficult decision, Laurier suggested that Canada create its own navy.

YES TO THE NAVY

Laurier proposed to create a Canadian navy of five cruisers and six destroyers. With Parliament's approval, the navy could be loaned to Britain if needed and would consist of volunteers. Canada would thus not be forced into British imperialist wars, as French Canadians feared, and would be able to help Britain in times of need, as English Canadians wanted.

NO TO THE NAVY

Many English Canadians laughed at the "tin pot navy" that would be too small and too out-of-date to be of any help. Canada did not need protection, they argued. Conservative leader Robert Borden demanded that money be immediately given to Great Britain so that it could purchase two dreadnoughts.

THE RESULT

Although Laurier's compromise did not convince either extreme, with a united party behind him, Canada's first navy was created in April 1910. In the federal election the next year, however, many French Canadians accused Laurier of giving in to the British, and Borden became the next prime minister.

Under Laurier's leadership, the Liberals had several major accomplishments.

1. They created the Yukon Territory as well as the provinces of Alberta and Saskatchewan.
2. They developed a Canadian navy.
3. They established the Alaska boundary with the United States.
4. Construction was initiated on a second transcontinental railway.

Today, the Canadian navy serves both a domestic and an international role. It patrols Canada's waters and also protects Canadian interests in other parts of the world.

The National Transcontinental Railway began construction in 1905. When completed in 1913, it ran between Winnipeg, Manitoba, and Moncton, New Brunswick.

🍁 The Depression was a time of severe unemployment. The unemployed often staged demonstrations to protest the lack of available jobs.

Reshaping Canada, 1921–1948

King successfully pushed for each British colony to have control over its own foreign policy.

The First World War reshaped Canadian politics. Prime Minister Robert Borden's decision in 1917 to make military service compulsory alienated French Canada from the Conservative Party. As a result, four years later, the Liberal Party under William Lyon Mackenzie King swept into power.

In the 1925 election, neither the Liberal nor the Conservative parties won a majority government. However, Mackenzie King convinced the Progressives to support the Liberal Party and thus became prime minister of Canada's first **minority government**.

A corruption scandal rocked the government later that year, and King asked Governor General Lord Byng to dissolve parliament and call an election.

The Liberal Party won the election and formed a majority government.

In 1921, Britain controlled Canada's political and economic relations with other countries. King successfully pushed for each British colony to have control over its own foreign policy. In 1926, the Balfour Report gave equal status to each member of the **British Commonwealth of Nations**. Canada was now free to make its own decisions.

The Conservatives under R.B. Bennett won the 1930 election. This defeat was a stroke of luck for Mackenzie King. As the **Great Depression** worsened, Bennett got the blame. As a result, the Liberal Party returned to power in 1935 and remained there through the Depression, the Second World War, and the post-war period to 1957.

THE CHANAK CRISIS

Following World War I, the Allies forced Turkey to sign the Treaty of Sèvres. Turkey was forced to give up Iraq, Syria, Lebanon, and some Aegean islands. The Dardanelles, a strait leading to the Aegean Sea, was to be demilitarized. In October 1922, Turkish troops threatened British troops stationed near Chanak on the Dardanelles. In response, the British government asked its colonies for military support.

YES, HELP GREAT BRITAIN

Arthur Meighen, the Conservative leader, argued that Canada should support Great Britain. He quoted Laurier, saying "When Britain's message came, then Canada should have said, 'Ready, aye ready, we stand by you.'"

NO, DO NOT SEND TROOPS

Mackenzie King believed that most Canadians did not want to get involved in another war. King also wanted to avoid being dragged into a war that would again divide English and French Canada. He wrote in his diary that he was "convinced that it is not right to take this country into another European war, and I shall resist to the uttermost."

THE RESULT

Instead of agreeing, as Canadian prime ministers were expected to do, King said that he would not send troops until Parliament decided. However, Parliament was on a break. By the time the issue had been debated in Parliament, the war was over. This was the beginning of the end of Canada always agreeing to British requests. At the 1923 and 1926 Imperial Conferences between Great Britain and its colonies, King successfully pushed for each colony to have control over its own foreign policy.

The Liberals had many achievements during the war years.

1. They established old age pensions, family allowances, and unemployment insurance.
2. They gained independence from Great Britain.
3. They helped create The National Film Board.
4. Under King, Canada become a founding member of the United Nations.

Since its creation in 1939, the National Film Board has been responsible for more than 13,000 productions.

Canada's role in both world wars broadened its visibility and reputation internationally. This helped the country achieve autonomy from Great Britain.

Post-War Politics, 1948–1967

The first decade after the Second World War was filled with confidence and prosperity. Prime Minister Louis St. Laurent thus had a relatively easy time winning the elections of 1949 and 1953.

On the foreign stage, St. Laurent took a more active role in international affairs. Canada joined **NATO**, and sent more than 22,000 soldiers to fight in the Korean War (1950-1953). In 1957, the United States and Canada built a long line of radar stations from Alaska to Baffin Island to watch for Soviet missiles and aircraft.

In 1957, after 22 years in office, the Liberals lost a close election to John Diefenbaker's Conservative Party. The Liberals took 105 seats to the Conservatives' 112. It was Canada's first minority government since 1925. St. Laurent retired from politics shortly after the election.

Lester Pearson, a recent Nobel Peace Prize winner, became the new party leader. Full of confidence, Pearson immediately demanded that the Conservative Party relinquish power. Diefenbaker ridiculed the idea and called an election, which his party won in the largest landslide in Canadian history to that time.

Pearson set about rebuilding the Liberal Party by bringing in new blood and adopting new policies. As a result, the Liberals narrowly lost the 1962 election. A crisis involving arming Canada with nuclear weapons brought the Liberals back to power in 1963—although with a minority government. The Liberal Party won another minority government in 1965.

> **In 1957, after 22 years in office, the Liberals lost a close election to John Diefenbaker's Conservative Party.**

❧ Canada's armed forces continue to play an important role in NATO operations, including anti-piracy missions in the Middle East.

CHOOSING A FLAG

Soon after Lester Pearson was elected in 1963, he asked Canadians to submit their ideas to the government's flag committee. Pearson's decision to adopt a Canadian flag divided Canadians between those who wanted to keep the British Red Ensign, which was Canada's unofficial flag, and those who wanted a new flag.

A NEW FLAG

Pearson wanted a distinctive flag to promote national unity. "Under this flag," he stated, "may our youth find new inspiration for loyalty to Canada; for a patriotism…that all Canadians will feel for every part of this good land." In 1958, more than 80 percent of Canadians surveyed had said they wanted a flag that was not already flown by another country.

THE RED ENSIGN

Conservative leader John Diefenbaker favoured keeping the Red Ensign as it was a symbol of Canada's ties to Great Britain. When it became clear that the public desired a new flag, Diefenbaker wanted one that honoured Canada's British heritage. He insisted that Great Britain's flag, the Union Jack, be incorporated into the design.

THE RESULT

The debate in Parliament dragged on for 98 days. Diefenbaker and his supporters made 250 speeches on the issue. The government was brought to a standstill. Finally, Pearson used **closure** to put an end to the debate. In February 1965, the red maple leaf on its red and white banner became Canada's official flag.

In the post-war years, the Liberal Party continued its list of achievements.

1. Under St. Laurent, the Liberals created the National Library of Canada, and the Canada Council for the Arts.
2. The party also helped establish NATO and the St. Lawrence Seaway.
3. Under Pearson, the Liberals established **universal health care** and the Canada Pension Plan. The party also unified the armed forces and created a national flag.

The St. Lawrence Seaway extends from Montreal to Lake Erie. Today, it is part of a larger system called the Great Lakes St. Lawrence Seaway. This larger seaway is 3,700 kilometres and extends all the way from the Atlantic Ocean to Lake Superior.

The Canada Council's mandate is to foster the enjoyment and creation of artistic works in areas including music, dance, and theatre.

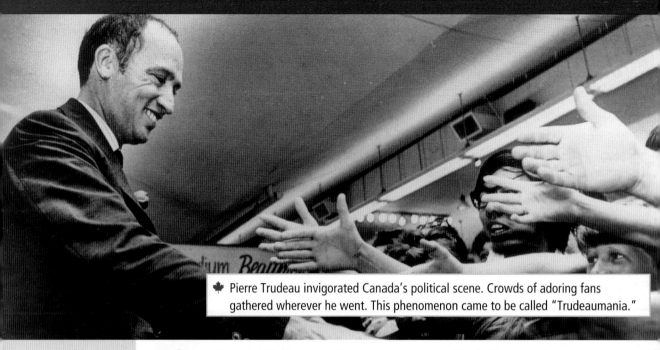

🍁 Pierre Trudeau invigorated Canada's political scene. Crowds of adoring fans gathered wherever he went. This phenomenon came to be called "Trudeaumania."

The Exciting Years, 1968–1984

In 1968, Canadians wanted fresh political faces to lead them. Pierre Elliott Trudeau seemed ideal. He was handsome, witty, intelligent, and an exciting speaker. People were impressed by Trudeau's vision of what he termed "a **just society**."

As part of this vision, his government passed the 1969 Official Languages Act. The act gave French and English Canadians equal status in the courts, in Parliament, and in government services. It also made French and English the official languages of Canada. Trudeau hoped that the promotion of bilingualism would stop demands for an independent Quebec.

However, in 1980, René Lévesque's Parti Québécois (PQ) held a **referendum** on leaving Confederation. Trudeau used his personal popularity in the province to persuade Quebecers to remain in Canada. On referendum day, almost 60 percent of the province voted to remain in Canada.

Trudeau then began to push for a new Canadian Constitution. He wanted to

patriate Canada's Constitution and include a Charter of Canadian Rights and Freedoms in the Constitution to ensure that everyone's individual rights were protected. After 18 months, he succeeded.

Trudeau resigned as prime minister and party leader in 1984, and John Turner was elected the new Liberal leader. Turner called an immediate election. When Turner made several controversial appointments just before the election, Conservative leader Brian Mulroney attacked him as another corrupt politician. The voters believed Mulroney, and the Liberals suffered a devastating defeat. John Turner had been prime minister for only 80 days.

Turner slowly rebuilt the Liberal Party. In the 1988 election, he opposed the Conservative Free Trade Agreement with the United States on **nationalistic** grounds. Although the party doubled its seats, Mulroney won again. Two years later, Turner resigned, and Jean Chrétien became the new Liberal Party leader.

> **People were impressed by Trudeau's vision of what he termed "a just society."**

INVOKING THE WAR MEASURES ACT

One of Pierre Trudeau's first challenges as prime minister was dealing with radical Quebec separatists. The Front de Libération du Québec (FLQ) believed that it could "free" Quebec through violent revolution. On October 5, 1970, four FLQ members kidnapped British diplomat James Cross from his Montreal home and threatened to execute him if their demands were not met. Five days later, the terrorists kidnapped Pierre Laporte, the Quebec minister of labour. To end the terrorism, Prime Minister Trudeau invoked the War Measures Act, giving police wide powers of search, arrest, and seizure. Not everyone agreed.

YES TO THE ACT

The police were frustrated by their inability to find the terrorists. Quebecers feared that the FLQ would strike again. To ensure the safety of Quebecers, Premier Robert Bourassa, with the unanimous support of the legislature, asked the federal government for help.

NO TO THE ACT

The Act had never been used during peace. As it gave the police special powers to search, question, and arrest suspects without cause, some Canadians argued that it was a threat to civil liberties. Others felt that invoking the act was an extreme measure for a minor crisis.

THE RESULT

When Trudeau invoked the War Measures Act to handle the situation, Montreal was placed under a curfew, and the army was called in to assist the police. Almost 500 people were arrested and held in custody for up to three weeks without being charged. Many were imprisoned merely on suspicion, and most were later released. The police found the body of Pierre Laporte and negotiated the release of James Cross. At their request, five FLQ terrorists were exiled to Cuba instead of facing trial.

Under Pierre Trudeau, the Liberals worked toward a just society of Canadians.

1. The Liberals patriated Canada's Constitution and developed the Canadian Charter of Rights and Freedoms.
2. They passed the Official Languages Act and the Multiculturalism Act.
3. They created Petro-Canada.
4. The Liberals established an immigration policy that eliminated discrimination.

On April 17, 1982, Queen Elizabeth II took part in the ceremony that patriated Canada's Constitution.

Petro-Canada was initially a Crown Corporation, which gave the Canadian government control over the energy sector. In 1991, it became a private sector company.

The Chrétien Years, 1990–2003

The 1993 election created a major political shift in the country. Although Chrétien's Liberal Party promised to create jobs, renegotiate the North American Free Trade Agreement (NAFTA), and repeal the Goods and Services Tax (GST), Canadians voted against the policies of previous Conservative government rather than for the Liberals. The Conservative Party under Kim Campbell almost disappeared. It elected only two members as the Liberal Party swept to power with 177 members.

The Liberal Party benefited from a revived economy and easily won the 1997 and 2000 elections. Under Finance Minister Paul Martin, the party balanced the federal budget and eliminated the $42 billion deficit it had inherited. Martin froze government wages, cut spending on defence, social services, and foreign aid, and reduced the number of government employees. To promote business opportunities in foreign markets, the Liberal Party established Team Canada Missions to Asia, South America, Mexico, Russia, and Germany.

On September 11, 2001, hijackers crashed two commercial jets into the twin towers of the World Trade Center in New York City. Nearly 3,000 people were killed, including 24 Canadians. The terrorist attack was blamed on Osama bin Laden and the terrorist group al-Qaeda.

When the United States attacked Afghanistan for providing refuge for bin Laden, Chrétien had to decide whether or not to participate. Almost a month later, he announced that Canadian armed forces would join the United States in the war in Afghanistan. Canada's initial contribution of ships, surveillance aircraft, and more than 2,000 armed forces members was the largest combat force it had sent abroad since the Korean War.

Change was in the air, however. In December 2003, Chrétien resigned as party leader and prime minister. The Liberal Party chose Paul Martin as his replacement.

> **When the United States attacked Afghanistan for providing refuge for bin Laden, Chrétien had to decide whether or not to participate.**

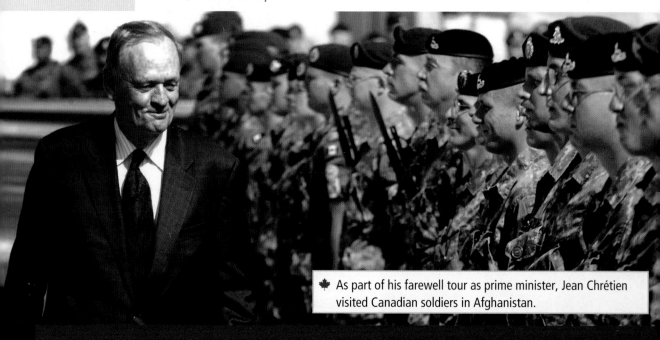

As part of his farewell tour as prime minister, Jean Chrétien visited Canadian soldiers in Afghanistan.

SHOULD QUEBEC SEPARATE?

When the Parti Québécois was re-elected in 1994, Premier Jacques Parizeau promised Quebecers a referendum on **sovereignty**. This referendum was held on October 30, 1995. This was the second referendum on independence. In 1980, the "No" side had defeated the sovereigntists with 59.6 per cent of the vote. Parizeau felt that the **separatist** movement now had enough support to win a referendum on Quebec separatism. Others fought to keep Quebec part of Canada.

YES TO SEPARATION

Many Quebecers felt that the province would be better able to meet its goals and maintain its unique culture if it was not part of Canada. There was simply too much interference from the federal government in these matters. Separating would be good for Quebec and its people.

NO TO SEPARATION

Those against separation countered that the unrest that Quebec experienced in 1980 had largely disappeared. Programs were now in place to improve conditions within the province, and these programs were working. If Quebec were to leave, many argued that it would be the end of Canada.

THE RESULT

The "No" side squeaked out a narrow 50.58 to 49.42 per cent victory. However, approximately 60 per cent of Francophones voted "Oui." Clearly, there was still work to be done to make Quebecers feel comfortable as Canadians.

The Chrétien government improved Canada's economic and political ties throughout the world.
1. It expanded the Free Trade Agreement with the United States to include Mexico.
2. It extended economic ties with the Pacific Rim countries.
3. It signed the Kyoto Protocol to lower greenhouse gas emissions.
4. It defeated the separatist referendum.

The House of Commons agreed to ratify the Kyoto Protocol in December 2002. Under the protocol, Canada agreed to reduce its greenhouse gas emissions by 6 percent by 2012.

The act under which Mexico joined the free trade alliance between Canada and the United States is called the North American Free Trade Agreement, or NAFTA. Since then, there have been several efforts to expand the agreement to include other nations in the Americas.

♦ The Gomery Commission held public hearings for about nine months. In that time, the commission interviewed 172 witnesses, including both Jean Chrétien and Paul Martin.

The Years in Exile, 2003-2011

Almost as soon as Paul Martin became prime minister in December 2003, the Liberal Party became entangled in a scandal involving the misuse of money in Quebec. Canada's Auditor General reported that the government paid more than $100 million to companies in Quebec for doing little or no work. Martin appointed Justice Charles Gomery to investigate the "sponsorship scandal," and called a snap election for June 2004.

Dion inherited a party that was disorganized, deeply in debt, and suffering from low morale.

The Liberal Party won only 135 of 308 seats and formed a minority government. Although the Gomery Commission cleared Martin in late 2005, the opposition blamed Martin because he had been minister of finance and, in their opinion, should have known where the money was going. When the opposition forced an election in January 2006, Martin was defeated by Stephen Harper's Conservative Party. Martin resigned as party leader.

The Liberal Party elected Stéphane Dion to replace Martin. Dion had a stellar history with the party, but was unable to generate much excitement in the party. During the 2008 election campaign, Harper successfully cast doubts on Dion's leadership abilities. As a result, the party was reduced to 76 seats, and Dion announced that he would resign as party leader.

Following Dion's resignation in December 2008, Michael Ignatieff became leader. Although the Conservatives had a minority government, Ignatieff twice failed to force an election in 2009. His effectiveness as a leader became an issue both within the party and among the voting public. When an election was finally called in 2011, the Liberals had their worst defeat ever, losing 43 of their 77 seats to finish in third place. Ignatieff lost his own seat and resigned as party leader. He was replaced by interim leader, Bob Rae.

MARTIN AND THE SPONSORSHIP SCANDAL

In 2004, Auditor General Sheila Fraser reported that the Liberal government had paid more than $100 million to Quebec companies for doing little or no work to promote national unity. Paul Martin, who had succeeded Chrétien, appointed Charles Gomery to investigate the "sponsorship scandal." In the January 2006 election, the issue was clear—should Martin be blamed for the scandal?

YES

The opposition parties claimed that, as minister of finance, Martin should have known where the money was going. The NDP asked voters not to reward Martin and the Liberal Party. Stephen Harper asked, "Do Canadians really believe that the No. 2 man in a government, now under a cloud of corruption, is the person to clean up that mess today?"

NO

The Gomery Commission cleared Martin of all wrongdoing, saying that Chrétien kept most of his cabinet, including finance minister Paul Martin, in the dark. Martin promised that the party would repay the money, moved to expel 10 guilty people from the party, and turned the inquiry's findings over to the RCMP.

THE RESULT

The election resulted in a Conservative minority government. The defeat ended 12 straight years of Liberal rule in Canada and Martin soon resigned. Because the Conservatives picked up 10 seats in Quebec, Stephen Harper claimed that the scandal had inflicted "enormous damage to the image of federalism" in Quebec.

Liberal Legacy

The Liberals had plans to improve various social issues. These plans were not implemented due to the short term in office.

1. The Liberals put together a health care deal that was to provide billions of dollars in funding to the provinces.
2. After meeting with Aboriginal leaders, the Martin government pledged long-term funding for Aboriginal development.
3. The Liberals pledged a not-for-profit national childcare program.

Under Martin's child care program, the government subsidized parents who wanted to put their children in daycare. Parents paid lower daycare fees as a result.

Since leaving office, Paul Martin has continued to support Aboriginal causes. He has developed programs designed to encourage Aboriginals to seek post-secondary education and to establish their own businesses.

TIMELINE

D ue to its long history in Canada, the Liberal Party has long held a dominant position in the country. As a result, it has contributed much to the country's development. Still, along with its successes, the party has also experienced many challenges—some of which have been easier to overcome than others. The timeline below summarizes some of the key moments in the Liberal Party's history.

1837

1861 The Liberal Party is created in the Canadas.

1867 Confederation creates a country called Canada.

Rebellions take place as reformers fight for greater democracy in the Canadas.

1873 As a result of the Pacific Scandal, the Liberal Party under Alexander Mackenzie comes to power.

1890 Manitoba abolishes French as an official language.

1896 Wilfrid Laurier becomes the country's first French-Canadian prime minister.

1911 Laurier and the Liberals are defeated.

1914-18 First World War

1917 The issue of conscription divides the country and weakens the Liberal Party.

1921 William Lyon Mackenzie King becomes prime minister.

1922 Under King, Canada refuses Great Britain's request to send troops to the Chanak region of the Dardanelles.

1929 The Liberals lose the election as the Great Depression begins.

1935 The Liberals return to power.

1939-45 Second World War

1942 King decides against conscription after holding a referendum on the issue.

1948

King resigns as prime minister and is replaced by Louis St. Laurent.

1950-53

Korean War

1957

Conservative John Diefenbaker ends the long Liberal control of Parliament.

1965

Lester Pearson approves the maple leaf flag.

1967

French President Charles de Gaulle visits Canada and promotes Quebec independence. Pearson denounces his actions.

1968

Pierre Elliott Trudeau is elected prime minister.

1969

Parliament passes the Official Languages Act.

1970

The FLQ kidnaps a British diplomat during the October Crisis. Trudeau enacts the War Measures Act in response.

1980

Quebec holds a separatist referendum. Trudeau uses his influence to support the "No" side.

1993

Jean Chrétien becomes prime minister as the Conservative Party is decimated.

1995

The second Quebec separatist referendum is held. The **federalists** win by a slim margin.

2001

The World Trade Center is hit by terrorist planes. Chrétien pledges Canada's support in the war on terrorism.

2004

The sponsorship scandal negatively impacts the reputation of the Liberal Party.

10 FAST FACTS
ABOUT THE LIBERAL PARTY

2 The Liberal Party is the oldest continuously running political party in Canada.

1 At one time, the Liberals were called the Grits. The name comes from the term Clear Grit, which was a type of sand used to make mortar.

3 Wilfrid Laurier is one of only two prime ministers to have won four consecutive majorities. The other is Conservative prime minister, John A. Macdonald.

4 Under King and St. Laurent, more immigrants came to Canada than at any time since 1913. As a result, Canada began to lose its largely British and French nature. The government introduced the sponsorship system that allowed Canadian residents to sponsor dependent relatives wishing to immigrate to Canada. Canada also accepted refugees fleeing from political oppression in Eastern Europe.

5 The Liberal Party was the first to hold a convention to elect a leader, Mackenzie King, in 1919.

6 Under the Liberal Party, Canada was the first Commonwealth country to create its own citizenship. At the first Canadian citizenship ceremony in 1947, King received citizenship certificate number 0001.

7 The first four leaders of the Liberal Party chosen by national leadership conventions, W.L. Mackenzie King (1919), Louis St. Laurent (1948), Lester Pearson (1958), and Pierre Elliott Trudeau (1968), were "outsiders" who had not served in the House of Commons for many years.

8 The Canadian Press named Pierre Trudeau "Newsmaker of the Year" a record 10 times and declared him "Newsmaker of the 20th Century."

9 In the 2008 election, a record 22.4 percent of the successful ministers of parliament were women. One-quarter of the successful Liberal candidates were women. The Liberal Party had the highest proportion of women candidates at 36.8 percent.

10 The Liberal Party has had more years in power than any other political party in Canada. In the 20th century alone, it held power for almost 69 years.

ACTIVITY

WHAT IS A DEBATE?

When people debate a topic, two sides take a different viewpoint about one idea. They present logical arguments to support their views. Usually, each person or team is given a set amount of time to present its case. The presenters take turns stating their arguments until the total time set aside for the debate is used up. Sometimes, there is an audience in the room listening to the presentations. Later, the members of the audience vote for the person or team they think made the most persuasive arguments.

Debating is an important skill. It helps people to think about ideas thoughtfully and carefully. It also helps them develop rhythms of speech that others can follow easily.

Some schools have organized debating clubs as part of their after-school activities. Schools often hold debates in their history class or as part of studying about world events.

DEBATE THIS!

Every day, the news is filled with the issues facing Canada and its citizens. These issues are debated in the House of Commons and on city streets. People often have different views of these issues and support different solutions.

Following is an issue that has sparked discussion across the country. Gather your friends or classmates, and divide into two teams to debate the issue. Each team should take time to properly research the issue and develop solid arguments for their side.

Canada is known worldwide for its universal health care program. This is a government-funded program that ensures health care for every Canadian who needs it. In recent years, however, the health care system has become overloaded. There are not enough medical facilities for everyone who needs care. Wait times for appointments and surgeries have increased as a result. There has been growing support for private health care programs for those who can afford them. People who could afford their own care could skip the lines at public hospitals and go to private hospitals with their health concerns.

This raises the question: Should the Canadian government introduce a two-tiered health care system, with both private and public hospitals?

QUIZ

1. To what group can the Liberals trace their beginnings?

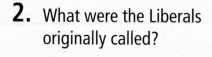

2. What were the Liberals originally called?

3. Who was the first leader of the Liberal Party?

4. Which Liberal prime minister was responsible for creating Canada's navy?

5. What was the Balfour Report?

6. Which Liberal prime minister was also a Nobel Peace Prize winner?

7. Which Liberal leader campaigned for Canada to be "a just society"?

8. What was the FLQ?

9. Which Liberal prime minister decided that Canada would join the United States in its war against terrorism?

10. What was the role of the Gomery Commission?

FURTHER RESEARCH

Suggested Reading

Brooke, Jeffrey. *Divided Loyalties: The Liberal Party of Canada, 1984–2008*. Toronto: University of Toronto Press, 2010.

Clarkson, Stephen. *The Big Red Machine*. Vancouver: University of British Columbia Press, 2005.

Goldenberg, Eddie. *The Way It Works*. Toronto: Douglas Gibson Books, 2006.

Internet Resources

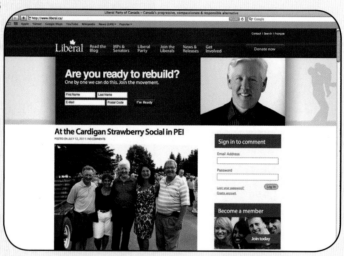

Read about the Liberal Party of Canada directly from the source at **www.liberal.ca**

A detailed history of the Liberal Party can be found at **www.thecanadianencyclopedia.com**. Just type Liberal Party into the search engine.

Learn more about Canada's political parties and the election process at **www.elections.ca**

GLOSSARY

British Commonwealth of Nations: an association of nations consisting of the United Kingdom and several former British colonies that are now sovereign states but still pay allegiance to the British Crown

closure: a procedure by which debate may be halted and an immediate vote taken

colonies: regions ruled by a country that is usually far away

Confederation: the event in 1867 when Canada became its own country, the original four provinces were Quebec, Ontario, Nova Scotia, and New Brunswick

conscription: mandatory military service

democracy: a political system in which the people elect the members of government

diplomacy: skill in the management of international relations

economic depression: a period of high unemployment and low sales of products

federalists: people who support a system of government in which power is divided between a central authority and constituent political units

Great Depression: a period during the 1930s when there was a worldwide economic depression and mass unemployment

just society: a group that adheres to the morals and ethics of the majority rather than of a small ruling class

minority government: a government that has won half or fewer than half of the seats in the House of Commons

nationalistic: supporting national independence or a strong national government

NATO: North Atlantic Treaty Organization; an international organization composed of the U.S., Canada, Britain, and a number of European countries for purposes of collective security

Pacific Scandal: a political scandal in which the Conservative Party was accused of accepting bribes to influence the bidding for the construction of the Canadian Pacific Railway

patriate: to turn over full legislative powers

reciprocity: the mutual exchange of trading privileges

referendum: a legislative act is referred for final approval to a popular vote by the electorate

representative government: a political system in which the number of elected seats allowed to each region depends on the number of people living there

responsible government: a form of government in which decisions cannot become law without the support of the majority of elected representatives

separatist: people who support the idea of withdrawing a province from Confederation

sovereignty: complete independence and self-government

universal health care: a health insurance program that is financed by taxes and administered by the government to provide comprehensive health care that is accessible to all citizens of that nation

INDEX

Balfour Report 12, 28
Blake, Edward 5, 6, 8
Bloc Québécois 4
Brown, George 6, 8, 29

Chrétien, Jean 5, 6, 7, 16, 18, 19, 20, 21, 23, 29
Confederation 6, 8, 9, 16, 22
Conservative Party 4, 8, 10, 11, 12, 13, 14, 15, 16,
    18, 20, 21, 23, 24
constitution 5, 16, 17

Diefenbaker, John 14, 15, 23
Dion, Stéphane 6, 20

FLQ 17, 23, 29

Gomery Commission 20, 21, 29

Harper, Stephen 20, 21

Ignatieff, Michael 6, 20

King, William Lyon Mackenzie 5, 6, 12, 13, 22, 23,
    24, 25

Laurier, Wilfrid 5, 6, 8, 10, 11, 13, 22, 24, 29

Macdonald, John A. 8, 9, 24
Mackenzie, Alexander 5, 6, 8, 9, 22
Martin, Paul 5, 6, 18, 20, 21

New Democratic Party (NDP) 4, 21

Pacific Scandal 8, 22
Parti Québécois 16, 19
Pearson, Lester B. 5, 6, 7, 14, 15, 23, 25, 29
Progressive Party 4, 12

referendum 16, 19, 22, 23
reformers 8, 22, 29
responsible government 4, 8

St. Laurent, Louis 6, 14, 15, 23, 24, 25

Trudeau, Pierre Elliott 5, 6, 7, 16, 17, 23, 25, 29
Turner, John 6, 16